UNSPEAKABLE IF...

for Heather

UNSPEAKABLE IF...

Steve Bell

methuen

1 3 5 7 9 10 8 6 4 2

Published in 2003 by Methuen Publishing Ltd
215 Vauxhall Bridge Rd, London SW1V 1EJ
www.methuen.co.uk

Copyright © 2003 Steve Bell

The right of Steve Bell to be identified as author of this work has been asserted
by him in accordance with the Copyright, Designs and Patents Act 1988

Illustrations © 2001, 2002, 2003 Steve Bell

Methuen Publishing Limited Reg. No. 3543167

A CIP catalogue record for this book is available from the British Library

ISBN 0 412 77357 4

Designed by Brian Homer and Jim Deaves

Printed and bound in India by Repro India Limited, Mumbai

Contents

Once Upon A Time, Before The World Changed

There was a cute, innocent monkey who only wanted to be allowed the freedom to develop Weapons of Mass Destruction in Deep Space where they couldn't possibly hurt anybody. It was a happy time, a golden time and George The Monkey – who hadn't hurt anybody and who hadn't even been elected by anybody except the US Supreme Court, and who liked only trees, bananas and Big Oil – had a dream, and the dream was called 'Son Of Star Wars'. He came to Europe to tell them about his dream, but the Europeans laughed at him...

Rogue Farting Sheep

Ten years after the collapse of the evil Soviet Empire and the coming of the New World Order, America still felt insecure.

18.6.2001

Tories For Sale

When William Hague stood down as Conservative Party leader he left the field wide open for a contest between the ambitious Michael Portillo, the pugnacious David Davis, the ludicrous Iain Duncan Smith, the well-connected Michael Ancram and the well-upholstered Kenneth Clarke.

25.6.2001

11

A Job For The Boy

Beside the monetary cost of the monarchy, the emotional price is harder to gauge. Prince Edward's media career was fraught with difficulty.

2.7.2001

13

The Dissolute Approach

As the Tory leadership contest heated up, ex-minister Peter Lilley called for the legalisation of cannabis. In a benign fog of good vibes and sound judgement the party members decided to elect Iain Duncan Smith as leader.

9.7.2001

KEN – YOU GOT ANY **STRAIGHTS?** I NEED TO **ROLL A NUMBER**

STRAIGHT?! WHU...? COURSE I'M STRAIGHT! GETAWAY FROM ME!

CHILLOUT MAN – YOU GOT ONE STICKIN' OUT YER **NOSE!**

JUST LEND US ONE. I NEED TO **GET MELLOW** WITH **EXTREME PREJUDICE!**

© Steve Bell '01

MIRROR MIRROR ON THE WALL WHO IS THE **BIGGEST TORY** OF ALL?

BUNTER, KILLER, FATARSE, BIGLIPS AND **MAN WITH NO HAIR** – THE BIGGEST TORY IS **TONY BLAIR!**

EVERY DAY IN EVERY WAY, I, DUNCAN SMITH AM GETTING MORE AND MORE NORMAL!

I, DUNCAN SMITH – THE SLAPHEAD'S **SLAPHEAD!**

I, DUNCAN SMITH – THE LIPS OF **MARILYN MONROE** AND THE EYES OF **NORMAN TEBBIT!**

I, DUNCAN SMITH – THE **MAIN MAN** FOR THE **MAINSTREAM!**

The Day War
Broke Out

War With Abroad

The devastating attack on the World Trade Center in New York on Tuesday September 11th brought about a profound change in the American President. He ceased to be a figure of fun and became a World Statesman overnight. Strangely, though, he continued to look, walk, talk and act like a chimpanzee.

17.9.2001

Where Goats Dare

Osama Bin Laden and Al Qa'eda, his fanatical troupe of Islamic suicide bombers, were in the frame for the attack on the World Trade Center. While the US found it difficult to attack the idea of anti-Americanism which seemed to have taken hold across the Muslim world, Afghanistan, where the Taleban had played host to Bin Laden, presented a much likelier target.

24.9.2001

Where Goats Dare 2

As the good book says, 'And He shall set the sheep on His right hand, but the goats on the left' (Matthew 25:33). But first you have to find the tricky little bastards.

1.10.2001

WHERE GOATS DARE

-3.10.49-3-

GOTAMA TIN CANMEN — WHAT'S YOUR MOTIVATION HERE?

I ONLY WISH TO BRING PEACE BY ENFORCING THE FUNDAMENTALIST GOAT LIFESTYLE ACROSS THE PLANET.

WHAT DOES THAT INVOLVE?

① ONLY TIN CANS TO BE EATEN DURING THE HOURS OF DAYLIGHT
② ALL SHEEP TO WEAR A BAG OVER THEIR HEAD!

© Steve Bell 2001

WHERE GOATS DARE

-4.10.49-4-

THE EXCLUSIVE INTERVIEW WITH GOTAMA TIN CANMEN CONTINUES...

...⑰ HOLY WAR AGAINST ELEPHANTS
⑱ ELEPHANTS OUT OF GOAT'S HOLY PLACES

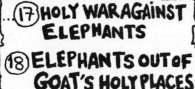

⑲ WHERE ARE A GOAT'S HOLY PLACES??

© Steve Bell '01

⑳ MY UNDERPANTS FOR A START!

WHERE GOATS DARE

-5.10.49-5-

THE ELEPHANTINE FORCES OF WESTERN DEVILMENT WILL NEVER DEFEAT ME!

I STAND HERE — A SIMPLE GOAT WITH NOTHING BUT A HOLE IN THE GROUND AND A LOVE OF FINE FURNISHINGS!

SEND IN MISSILES, SEND IN A MILLION ELEPHANTS! THEY WILL SIMPLY MAKE MY HOLE...

...BIGGER!

THANKS TO HUGH!

The Hunchback of Nostradamus

What with all the apocalyptic stuff in the news, the writings of the famous sixteenth century cleric came back into fashion. Unaccountably he was a year out in his predictions for the Hammers.

8.10.2001

A Sought-After Cave

The search for the legendary cave of Bin Laden went on as the war in Afghanistan got under way.

15.10.2001

27

Don't Panic, You Old Bag!

At home the fevered atmosphere was soothed by speculation about biological warfare. In Afghanistan fully grown male journalists went over the top in burkas.

22.10.2001

THAT'S QUITE ENOUGH **ANTHRAX** FOR NOW..... I NEED SOME **DEEP BACKGROUND** BARRY...

© Steve Bell 2001

DO ME A PROFILE OF THAT **MULLAH OMAR** — WHAT IS IT MAKES HIM **TICK**?

YOU MEAN THE...

ONE EYED BEARDED NONCE FROM HELL?

I'LL ASK AROUND...

ANY WORD FROM OUR MAN ON THE **FRONTLINE**...

...**BILLY BOLLOCKS**, THE **BLOKE IN THE BURKA**?

FACKIN' FACK! ME FACKIN' **SATELLITE PHONE**!

...I FINK IT'S **FACKED**!

WRITHE

CLANK

© Steve Bell 2001

BILLY BOLLOCKS, OUR **BLOKE IN THE BURKA** HAS DONE US **PROUD**!

THESE PICTURES ARE **FANTASTIC** — AND HE ONLY TOOK 'EM **TEN MINUTES AGO**!

WHAT'S THAT **THING** IN THE MIDDLE ??

IT'S SOME KIND OF **GREENBLOB**

© Steve Bell 2001

Billy Bollocks Goes In

Speculation as to the whereabouts of Osama Bin Laden, the soft-spoken psychopath with come-to-bed eyes, microscopic genitalia and a whopping great AK47 continued unabated.

29.10.2001

Billy Bollocks Goes Off

The war in Afghanistan was already proving to be one of the most dangerous ones ever for journalists.

5.11.2001

INSIDE BILLY BOLLOCKS

① SNUG INSIDE HIS BURKA BILLY BOLLOCKS PUTS ON VIRTUAL REALITY HEADSET DROPPED BY B52s....

② VIRTUAL REALITY HEADSET STIMULATES SOUND EFFECTS SOFTWARE HARD WIRED INTO BILLY BOLLOCKS' CEREBRAL CORTEX

④ BB ACCIDENTALLY VAPORISED BY OFF-COURSE BLU-82 FUEL AIR 'DAISY CUTTER'

EEEYOWW EEEYOWW

③ BB ARTICULATES IN REAL TIME

DAKKA DAKKA DAKKA

© Steve Bell 2001

7·11·4998·

STILL NO NEWS FROM BILLY BOLLOCKS, OUR BLOKE IN THE BURKA...

...I BEGINNING TO GET AN UNEASY FEELING ABOUT ALL THIS.... I THINK WE MUST FACE UP TO WHAT MAY HAVE HAPPENED

I FINK YOU'RE RIGHT

© Steve Bell '01

·8·11·4999·

BILLY BOLLOCKS - "I AM FIRST MAN INTO PARADISE"

CLUTCHING MY BOTTOMLESS G. AND T. I AM FORCED TO FIGHT OFF WILLING VIRGINS

ARTISTS' IMPRESSION

9·11·5000

WHAT'S THIS 'BLU-82 DAISY CUTTER' BARRY?

I FINK IT'S A WEAPON, HARRINA

BUSH DEMANDS MORE WHACK PER WEAPON

YES, BUT WHAT DOES IT DO?

FACT - IT'S AS BIG AS A CAR - 15000 lb !!

FACT - IT VAPORIZES AS IT SWEEPS AS IT CLEANS

JANE'S BANGING BOMBS

FACT - YOU DON'T FEEL A THING!

FACT - IT LEAVES NO TELL-TALE CORPOREAL REMAINS - SOUNDS LIKE EVERY GARDENER-PSYCHOPATH'S DREAM!!

JANE

© Steve Bell 2001

33

Northern Alliance

As the Taleban forces crumbled in the face of the US onslaught, the Northern Alliance of approved warlords and tractable Taleban moved in to fill the power vacuum.

12.11.2001

The Rumsfeld Follies

One of the most hawk-like hawks was US Defence Secretary Donald Rumsfeld. His style was a finely balanced blend of Crippen, Himmler and John Wayne.

19.11.2001

WITH THE SPECIAL FORCES:

THIS PLACE IS CRAZY!

IT'S FULL OF THINGS THAT GO BANG AND PEOPLE TRYING TO KILL EACH OTHER!

YOU HEARD THE RUMOUR?

WHAT RUMOUR?

BIN LADEN IS LYING LOW IN THE PARADISE ISLAND OF BALI!

LET'S GET OUTA THIS SHITHOLE PRONTO!

BOING

@Steve Bell '01

5008·21·11·

THE SIXTH SENSE SICKO

5009 22·11

THANKS TO TOM McMASTER·

@Steve Bell 01

I'M A LITTLE GUY WITH A BIG PROBLEM...

WHAT IS IT GEORGE? YOU TELL ME NOW, GEORGE, IN YOUR OWN WORDS

I DON'T SEE DEAD PEOPLE!

THE SIXTH SENSE SICKO

23·11· 5010·

WHY DON'T YOU THINK YOU CAN SEE DEAD PEOPLE, GEORGE?

I DON'T KNOW..... ...IT'S LIKE...

...THEY'RE TRYING NOT TO TELL ME SOMETHING

@Steve Bell 2001

WHAT DO YOU THINK IT IS THAT THEY'RE TRYING NOT TO TELL YOU?

THEY'RE TRYING NOT TO TELL ME THAT THEY'RE NOT DEAD AND I'M NOT A STUPID ASSHOLE

Gordon's Serenade

The Chancellor's Autumn Statement was packed with the promise of future spending.

26.11.2001

Bearded Sheep Alliance

At Mazar-i-Sharif, inside the personal stronghold of Northern Alliance leader General Dostum, hundreds of Taleban prisoners, many with their hands tied behind their backs, staged a revolt against their captors in which most of them died. One of the very few survivors turned out to be a native of California who had converted to Islam and gone off to fight with the Taleban.

3.12.2001

41

Tora Bora Boom Bang

The hunt for Osama Bin Laden centred in on a network of caves in the mountains of southern Afghanistan. He turned out to be somewhere else. Following the intensive destruction of the previous weeks the Americans proudly announced that they were 'not in the business of nation building'.

10.12.2001

42

Seek The Diamond in The Elephant's Ass

Sources close to the intelligence services disclosed that Osama Bin Laden was a passionate supporter of a well-known North London football club. This revelation didn't help to locate him, though.

17.12.2001

45

Sending Goats to Cuba

Many prisoners of war were sent to the specially prepared Camp X-Ray within the US Naval base at Guantanamo Bay on the island of Cuba. This was in direct contravention of the Geneva Convention.

14.1.2002

47

Royal Train Drug Shame

The cost of maintaining the Royal Train was in the spotlight. Meanwhile, in the USA after nearly choking to death on a pretzel, President Bush was in recovery.

21.1.2002

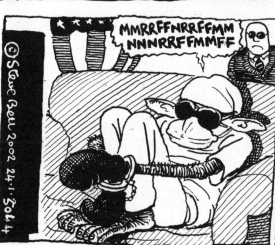

49

Enron: I Liked It So Much I Bought The Company

As Hamid Karzai, former oil executive and newly installed Prime Minister of Afghanistan visited Washington, the collapse of the giant energy corporation Enron caused a huge scandal.

28.1.2002

51

The Living Birdshit

A large marble statue of Margaret Thatcher was unveiled at the Guildhall in London.

4.2.2002

52

6·2·5053.

WHERE ARE WE GOING TO ERECT THIS THING?

I WAS THINKING...

...FACE DOWN IN THE THAMES?

NAH—IT'LL FRIGHTEN THE FISH!

HOW ABOUT AT THE END OF THE MAIN JOBBY DISPOSAL PIPE FOR THE THAMES BASIN?

7·2·5054

NAH—IT'LL FRIGHTEN THE RATS!

HOW ABOUT THE THIRD CIRCLE OF HELL?

NAH—IT'LL FRIGHTEN THE DEMONS!

I HAVE IT!—WE'LL SINK HER EXACTLY WHERE SHE SANK THE BELGRANO!!

NAH—THINK OF ALL THE INNOCENT WILDLIFE!

8·2·5055

THERE'S ONLY ONE PLACE FOR A RANCID MOUNTAIN OF CRAP LIKE THIS...

...THE CHAMBER OF THE HOUSE OF LORDS!

53

The Private Finance Initiative...

...or how I learned to stop worrying and love the banks. The audit company that recommended PFI was the same Arthur Andersen that audited Enron.

Tube Train Ken and Tony the Terror

The government was determined to impose the part-privatisation of the London Underground, against the wishes of London's elected Mayor Ken Livingstone.

11.2.2002

Corruption – Moi?

Tony Blair was contemptuous of any suggestion that his express support for New Labour backer Lakshmi Mittal's bid for control of the Romanian steel industry, against the wishes and interests of the UK steel industry, was in any way corrupt. Downing Street spin chiefs Powell and Campbell helped adjust the big picture.

18.2.2002

59

Tony and Silvio

Tony felt the need to get real with a visit to his multi-millionaire media-magnate pal, Silvio Berlusconi. At home, the hapless transport minister Stephen Byers succeeded in drawing attention away from his master's peccadilloes, while the Queen went off to Australia.

25.2.2002

61

The Queen Goes Down

The Governor General of Australia and former Archbishop Peter Hollingworth hosted the royal visit down under, where the Queen was greeted with a varied display of cultural festivity and sexual innuendo.

4.3.2002

63

The Plod's Plod

Britain's most senior and respected police officer sounded off about the state of the world.

11.3.2002

65

What Tony Believes In...

Tony Blair. In charge. For ever.

18.3.2002

The End of an Era

Margaret Thatcher announced publicly that she was no longer going to make any public announcements.

25.3.2002

69

Monkey World

The search for Tony Blair's core beliefs continued. George Bush Jr provided additional focus.
Meanwhile the Queen Mother died and the Penguin attempted to upstage her.

8.4.2002

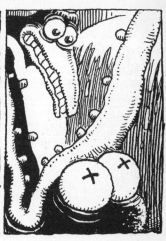

Death of a Penguin

The Lost Leader returned to his roots in the colonies.

15.4.2002

WHY WOULD THE **QUEEN'S** HUBBY WANT TO COME HERE?

NOT **THAT** PRINCE PHILIP, SIR...

...I MEAN THE **PENGUIN** PRINCE PHILIP OF GREECE — OUR **LOST LEADER**...

PAF!

...WHO LEGEND SAYS WILL RETURN TO **SAVE** US DURING THE **GLOBAL WAR ON ALBATROSS**

WE'D BETTER PUT OUR **BOW TIES** ON!

ARE WE ANYWHERE NEAR THE **DROP ZONE** YET, WING COMMANDER?

FIVE MINUTES TO GO, KIPLING

IT'S AWFULLY GOOD OF THE **RAF** TO PROVIDE FACILITIES FOR AN ESSENTIALLY **ANTI-IMPERIALIST STUNT**

ANYTHING CAN HAPPEN IN A **STRIP CARTOON**, OLD BOY!

I'M OPENING THE HATCH **NOW!**

SEE! HE COMES!

AWK! BUGGER!

IT'S BEEN AN **HONOUR KNOWING YOU**, PENGUIN...

FAREWELL OLD FRIEND!

SEE!

HE COMES!

SHIT! WHERE AM I?

73

Death of a Penguin 2

Despite the national outpouring of grief, the Lost Leader, transcending space and time, refused to die.

22.4.2002

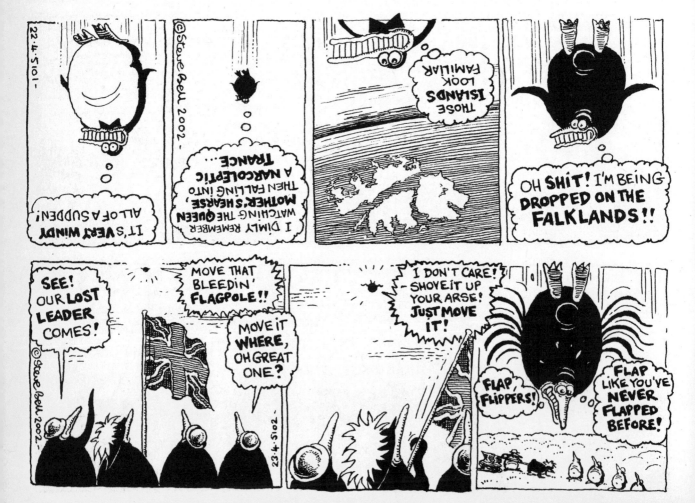

Five Years in Pah

Even after five whole years at the pinnacle of power, the search for the true meaning of Blairism went on and on.

29.4.2002

There's No Business Like Show Business

The Queen gave thanks for fifty glorious years on the throne with an all-marching all-honking drag review at the historic Westminster Hall.

1.5.2002

Adventures of Robo-Rat

Though the heat seemed to have died down somewhat, the search for Osama Bin Laden went on in strange new ways.

6.5.2002

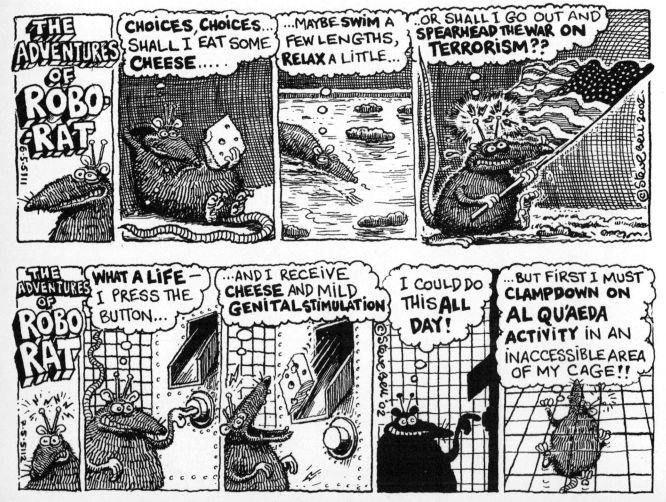

IN A PARTICULARLY REMOTE CORNER OF THE **HINDU KUSH:**

WHERE ARE WE, SERGEANT?

WE'RE IN A PARTICULARLY REMOTE CORNER OF THE **HINDU KUSH, SAH!**

WHY ARE WE HERE, SERGEANT?

WE'RE HERE TO **JUMP OUT OF HELICOPTERS, SAH!**

I'M SORRY SERGEANT — MY **MIND'S STARTING TO GO.** I THINK IT MAY BE **ALTITUDE SICKNESS**

THAT'S THE **OTHER REASON** WE'RE HERE, **SAH!**

WE'RE APPROACHING **HOSTILE HOLE IN THE GROUND** AT THE **ARSE END OF NOWHERE, SAH!**

LOOK! A PILE OF **RUBBLE!** THANK GOD THE **TELEVISION CAMERAS** ARE HERE!!

FORTUNATELY THIS TIME WE'RE READY — WE HAVE **THE MEANS** TO **ACCESS THE DARK PLACES BENEATH OUR FEET...**

WE HAVE **ROBO-RAT®** —TM—

GO, ROBO-RAT! SEEK OUT THE **HIDDEN FOE!**

GOD SPEED, ROBO-RAT!

FIFTEEN MINUTES LATER...

SQUEAK SQUEAK SQUEAKETY SQUEAK SQU-SQUEAK!!

SQUEAK!

WHAT'S HE SAYING SERGEANT?

81

Fat Sharon Up Gaza Toon

Three hundred and fifty pound stunner Ariel Sharon sought out a Middle East piece with his dancing partner and skin beauty consultant Shimon Peres.

13.5.2002

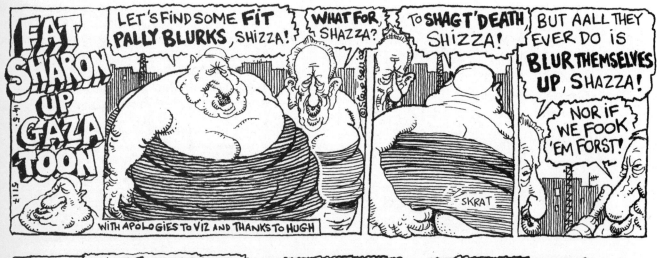

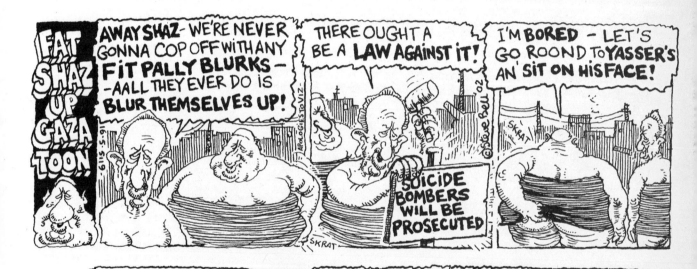

83

The Five Tests

At last Chancellor Gordon Brown revealed the precise nature of the legendary five tests for entry into the Single European Currency.

20.5.2002

85

The Royal Train

The truth was out: the Royal Train was on its last legs.

27.5.2002

The World Raw Fishball Cup

In faraway Japan and South Korea the World Cup got underway. The Swedes gave England an early fright, but the Argentinians and Nigerians succumbed to lashings of British Pluck. The French champions were unexpectedly overcome first by the Senegalese and then by the Danes.

10.6.2002

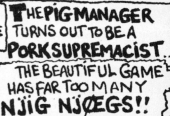

Offensive Accusations

In the run-up to the Queen's Golden Jubilee it was suggested that Tony Blair had attempted to acquire a more prominent role in the Queen Mother's funeral ceremony.

17.6.2002

The World Raw Fishball Cup 2

England's World Cup run came to an abrupt halt when it encountered the Brazilians. A determined but uninspired German team managed by Rudi Voller defeated the South Korean co-hosts. In the other semi-final the Brazilians saw off the Turks.

24.6.2002

WILL THE DOGS BE ABLE TO WITHSTAND...

...A STADIUM FILLED WITH MILLIONS OF **SCREAMING KING PRAWNS**....

EEEEEE
EEEEEE

ACH!! MEIN EAR-HOLES BLEEDING ARE!!

...AND A **SHIFTY CRAB** REFEREE?

NO PROBLEM — THEY'RE MANAGED BY A **MULLET**

26·6·5143

© Steve Bell '02

WHO WILL FACE THE DOGS IN THE WORLD RAW FISHBALL **CUP FINAL?**

VONE·NIL TO ZE HU·HU·HUNDS

VONE·NIL TO ZE HU·HU·HUNDS

WILL IT BE THE FLOWING, SEXY, MAGICAL, BUCK-TOOTHED PARROTS?

OR THE DETERMINED, DISCIPLINED AND **DEADLY GOATS?**

— © Steve Bell 2002

SCHEISSE! VE THE PARROTS FACE!

27·6·5144

THE DOGS PREPARE FOR THE **ULTIMATE SHOWDOWN** WITH THE **PARROTS**...

OLIVER KANINE — DU BIST DER ONLY PLAYER...

...MIT **VORLD CLASS** IN DIES ENTIRE BAG OF **SCHEISSHUNDS!**

CAN YOU SAVE **UNS** VON DIE **PARROTSTÜRM?**

JA, FISCHFOCHER, BUT ONLY IF YOU LOVE ME FOR **MYSELF** AND NICHT MEIN **GOAL-SCHTOPPING PROWESS!**

© Steve Bell 2002

93

People's Peerage for Hardnose

The oddest people were being elevated to the House of Lords for the unlikeliest of reasons. Harry Hardnose was a prime example, being honoured for services to mental health and international understanding.

1.7.2002

Government By The Oilmen For The Oilmen

As the idea of a follow-up war in Iraq took hold, George Bush Jr explained his rationale.

8.7.2002

Ultimate War Aims

As preparations were well under way it was time to check public opinion and get the story straight.

15.7.2002

99

Swamped by Pseudo-Afghans

In Australia the right-wing Howard government had made much of the threat from asylum seekers for purely electoral reasons.

22.7.2002

101

Drizzling Through

The Commonwealth Games began in Manchester. Nothing like it had been seen since the last Commonwealth Games.

29.7.2002

103

Return of the Crap Tanks

In the deserts of Oman a giant military exercise was taking place. As usual the dust played havoc with our gallant tanks.

5.8.2002

OVER THE TOP WITH THE CRAP TANKS

© Steve Bell 2002

NOW **FULLY DUSTICATED** AND **ANTI-HEATIFIED**, OUR TANKS ARE THE **ENVY** OF THE WORLD!

HEAT, DUST, WHATEVER YOU THROW AT US, SADDAM, **WE CAN TAKE IT!**

OH SHIT! FLIES!!

FORWARD WITH THE CRAP TANKS

© Steve Bell '02

I SUPPOSE WE MAY AS WELL **FACE IT**...

...**TANKS ARE CRAP!** THEY WON'T USE US AGAINST SADDAM BECAUSE **TANK ENGAGEMENTS** ARE A **THING OF THE PAST!!**

WHAT ABOUT **TANK WEDDINGS?**

ON HOLIDAY WITH THE CRAP TANKS

© Steve Bell '02

SUN, SAND, FLIES... THIS IS THE LIFE, EH CRAPPY?

FANCY A PADDLE?

I'B OBWAYS READY TO DO **PADDLE** AGAIDST THE **EDEBIES OB CIBILISATIOD!**

107

Strategic Dossiers

The evidence of Saddam Hussein's possession of Weapons of Mass Destruction just got bigger all the time.

16.9.2002

The Countryside Speaks

The Countryside Alliance claimed that 400,000 people attended its Liberty and Livelihood march through central London.

23.9.2002

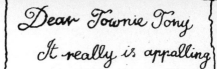

Bad Press for Charles

Having let slip the level of his support for fox hunting by suggesting that he might be forced to leave the country in order to spend his life skiing, Prince Charles was faced with an image problem.

30.9.2002

113

True Pants

Edwina Currie's memoirs, published just in time for the Party conference season, contained the staggering revelation that she had enjoyed a torrid affair with John Major back in the 1980s.

7.10.2002

115

New Adventures of Quietman

Iain Duncan Smith's speech to the Conservative Party conference in Bournemouth contained the shock warning: 'Never underestimate the determination of a quiet man.' The world caught its breath.

14.10.2002

117

World-Class Pimp

Jack Straw criss-crossed the Muslim world in a desperate attempt to solicit clients for the coalition of the willing to go to war against Iraq. He met with limited success.

21.10.2002

Deputy Dog

As Deputy Prime Minister John Prescott's star faded, so, in the office of Education Secretary, there arose an ugly new bruiser called Charles Clarke, who took over from the self-confessedly useless Estelle Morris.

28.10.2002

121

The Queen Is Clean

The court case against Princess Diana's former butler, Paul Burrell, collapsed spectacularly when the Queen let slip that she had known all along that he was looking after his former employer's knick-knacks for the benefit of posterity. Tony Blair confirmed the Queen's innocence.

4.11.2002

Buggering Butlers

The Burrell case brought to the surface tales of strange goings-on in the household of the Prince of Wales, who launched an inquiry spearheaded by one of his most trusted lackeys.

11.11.2002

Them Fookin' Firemen

John Prescott found himself at the head of a small group of politically motivated men dedicated to the overthrow of the firefighters' pay claim.

18.11.2002

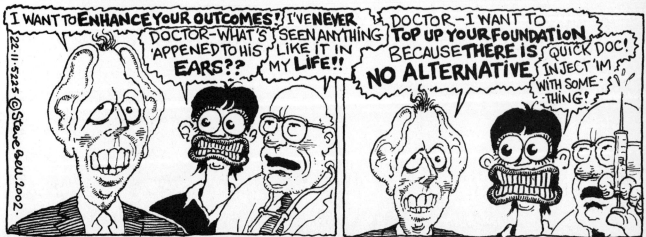

127

Do the
Shadow Cabinet
Re-Shuffle!

Ron and More Ron

People who questioned the intelligence and probity of the leader of the free world were making a fatal miscalculation.

25.11.2002

Doctor Sex

An expert in mass killing was clearly needed to lead an inquiry into the tragic events of September 11th. Henry Kissinger fitted the profile perfectly.

2.12.2002

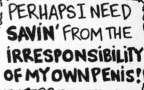

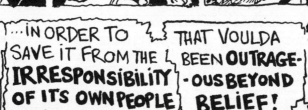

133

Third Way Tea

The boyfriend of Cherie Blair's personal New Age Bollocks consultant turned out to be a notorious Australian conman. The fact that he helped her with the purchase of two flats in Bristol for the use of her student son Euan supplied a very faint whiff of scandal.

16.12.2002

Old Modda Fokka's Almanack

A bloody drive-by shooting in Birmingham focused the nation's attention on the growing gun culture.

6.1.2003

137

Sharon Goes Pear Shaped

Ariel Sharon's Likud Party experienced a slight wobble in the Israeli general election campaign. Meanwhile in Farringdon Road the *Guardian*'s guidelines on the use of the word 'Fuck' were in turmoil.

13.1.2003

Move On Up to PFI

The Chancellor's predilection for off-balance-sheet solutions to his budget problems led to some interesting developments.

20.1.2003

AAH MABEL, DID YOU BRING THE **OFF-BALANCE-SHEET P.F.I. TEAPOT?**

NO, I BROUGHT THE **CONTRACT** FOR THE **OFF-BALANCE-SHEET P.F.I. TEAPOT**

AHHH! EXCELLENT!

HMMM... MIGHT NOT THESE CLAUSES HERE (27.1 THROUGH TO 34.8) PUT A **STRAIN ON THE EXCHEQUER?**

ONLY IF YOU SHOVE THEM UP YOUR ARSE, SIR

DEALING WITH THOSE **CONTRACTS** TOOK RATHER **LONGER THAN EXPECTED**....

...SO I'M REALLY **LOOKING FORWARD** TO MY **FIRST CUP** OF **OFF-BALANCE-SHEET P.F.I. TEA!!**

JINGS MABEL! WHY ARE YOU POURING **SCALDING WATER DOON MA LEGS!!**

CRIVENS WOMAN! YOU'VE **BILED MA KNACKERS!**

I HAVE NO OPTION BUT TO **WRING OOT MA TROOSERS** IN THIS CUP!

THIS **OFF-BALANCE-SHEET P.F.I TEA** HAS TURNED **BLUE!** JINGS! I THINK I'M GOING TO **FAINT!!**

MABEL! BRING ME THE **OFF-BALANCE-SHEET P.F.I. BISCUIT CONTRACTS** BEFORE I LAPSE INTO UNCONSCIOUSNESS!

I Hate Camels

President Bush delivered his second State of the Union speech. There was speculation as to how he would improve on the previous year's 'Axis of Evil' soundbite.

27.1.2003

Welcome to Hoon Island

The prospect of a massive demonstration against war in Iraq brought out the very best in the British Government. Defence Secretary Geoff Hoon and Culture Minister Tessa Jowell decided to impose a 'Keep Off The Grass' blockade in London's Royal Parks.

3.2.2003

145

Hot Intelligence

The British and American intelligence services were working flat out to uncover new justifications for the war on Iraq. Some corners were cut and some cut and paste facilities were abused.

10.2.2003

S.O.B.s with B.J.s

Two million people marched through London on February 15th, the biggest demonstration about anything ever in the UK. Tony Blair was not deflected from the path of righteousness.

17.2.2003

149

Noo Noocular Nukes

Always ahead of the game, the US defence industry came up with sophisticated new nuclear weapons of mass destruction, cleverly designed to seek out and destroy Weapons of Mass Destruction.

3.3.2003

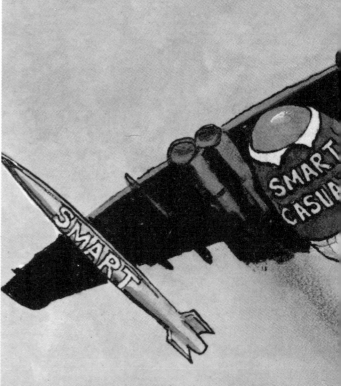

The Camels of MOAB

As the preordained window for war approached, stories began to circulate about the Mother Of All Bombs.

10.3.2003

154

THE BIG ORANGE **MOAB THING** IS THE **PRECURSOR** OF A CAMPAIGN TO **REFORGE THE MID-EAST**...

...**ESTABLISHING DEMOCRACY**, I BEG YOUR PARDON, **MOVING TOWARDS DEMOCRACY**.

...AND **LOOK! IT'S COMING** IN SMALL, INCREMENTAL STAGES...

...JUST LIKE A **CLUSTERBOMB**.

12·3·5283

©Steve Bell '03

13·3·5284

PHEW! JUST AS WELL THOSE **CLUSTER BOMBLETS** DIDN'T GO OFF!

THEY'RE **NOT SUPPOSED TO** THINK OF THEM AS **SEEDS OF DEMOCRACY** WAITING TO **GERMINATE!**

©Steve Bell '03

SOD THAT FOR A GAME OF SOLDIERS!

GO ON! RUN AWAY! YOU ARE **NO CAMEL!**

GALLOP GALLOP

14·3·5285

YOUR **HUMP** IS **CHEESE!**

GALLOP

©Steve Bell '03

DAMN YOUR MOTHER FOR A FRENCHWOMA...

KABLOOEY!

BAM

WHAM

155

World War Three Nostalgia

After the US and the UK failed to get a second resolution at the UN Security Council to legitimise the forthcoming conflict, Bush, Blair and José María Aznar of Spain met in the Azores for a council of war.

17.3.2003

Going In Twice

The war started slightly earlier than expected to allow a surprise 'decapitation' assault directly on the person of Saddam Hussein. No one was sure whether he was killed, wounded or unscathed, so there was much speculation as to whether the pictures of him broadcast on Iraqi TV were actually of one of his doubles.

24.3.2003

159

You're Fish!

In the waterways leading to the Iraqi port of Umm Qasr, teams of highly trained dolphins were set to work on mine-clearing duties. Some of them disappeared without leaving a forwarding address.

31.3.2003

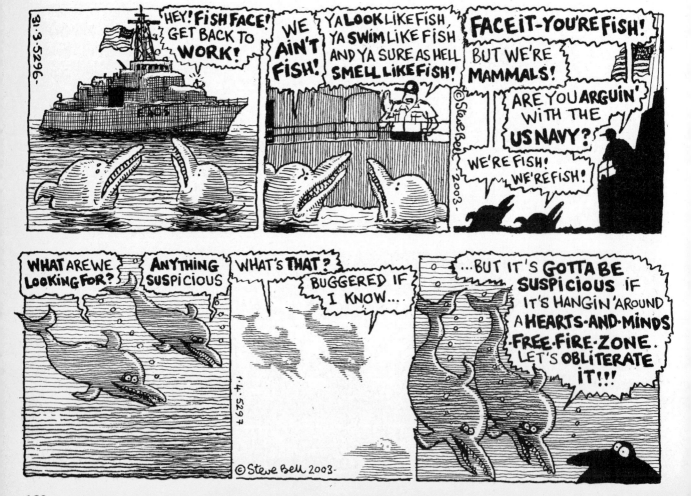

Checkpoint Charlies

As the war went into its second week, the number of 'friendly fire' incidents grew. So too did the number of civilians killed at road checkpoints by nervous, or perhaps simply trigger-happy soldiers.

7.4.2003

The Cradle of Civilisation

The expected last stand of the Iraqi Special Republican Guard failed to materialise, Baghdad fell to the Americans, the Iraqi regime evaporated, and looters took to the streets. As hospitals and museums were trashed, Donald Rumsfeld described the looting as an understandable reflex.

14.4.2003

Camp X-Club Juniors

It came to be known that certain inmates of the notorious Camp X-Ray in Guantanamo Bay were as young as thirteen.

28.4.2003

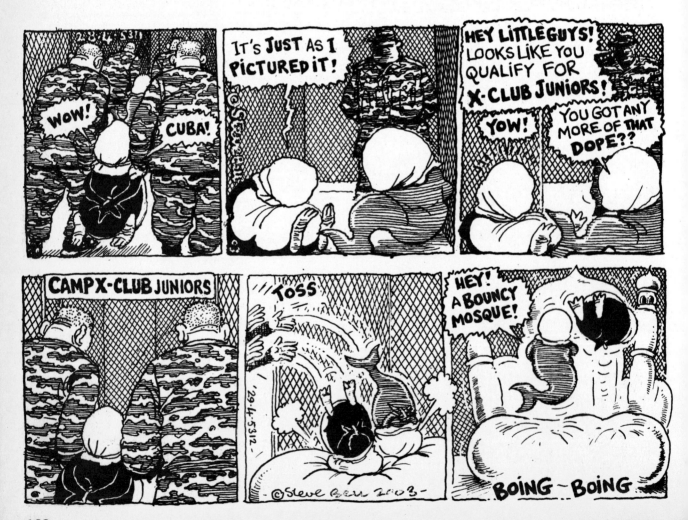

HEY - D'YOU WANT TO KNOW SOMETHING?

30·4·5313

CAMP X-RAY INFINITE TERROR CRÊCHE

WHAT'S THAT?

THERE ARE TWO COUNTRIES IN THE WORLD THAT HAVEN'T RATIFIED THE UN CONVENTION ON THE RIGHTS OF THE CHILD — SOMALIA AND THE USA!!

YOU HAVE TO MAKE ALLOWANCES FOR FAILED STATES!

©Steve Bell '03

IT'S THE TELETUBBIES!

...NO IT'S THE CHEMI-TUBBIES! THEY'RE LOOKING FOR WEAPONS OF MASS DESTRUCTION!

WHAT'S THIS GOT TO DO WITH US?

YOU TELL US, SHORT-BUTT!!

1·5·5314

PHEW! THE BAGS ARE OFF...AND THERE'S TV!

LET ME GET THIS STRAIGHT - WHETHER OR NOT WE SUPPLY EVIDENCE OF TERRORIST CRIMES, WE'RE STUCK HERE....

2·5·5315   ©Steve Bell '03

...BECAUSE WE'RE BEING HELD AS 'ENEMY COMBATANTS', WAR OR NO WAR?

DON'T ASK ME - I'M A SOLDIER NOT A LAWYER

CAN I SEE A LAWYER?

GET BACK ON THE CULTURALLY APPROPRIATE RECREATIONAL BOUNCY MOSQUE AND SHUT YOUR STUPID BEAK!!

167

The President Has Landed

George Bush, in full pilot's rig and monkey suit, co-piloted and landed a warplane on the flight-deck of the aircraft carrier 'Abraham Lincoln', fresh back from the Gulf, off the coast of California.

5.5.2003

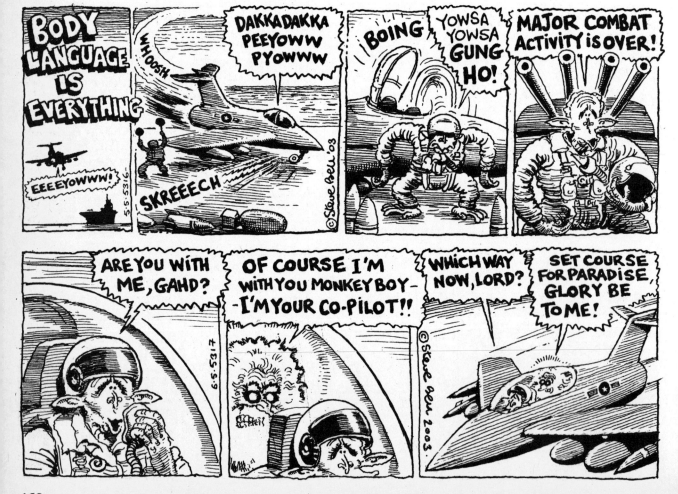

169

Saving Private Finance

Blair's mission to modernise was as fervent as ever. Firefighters, teachers, Clare Short, even Gordon Brown, all fell before his armed might.

12.5.2003

Stakeknife

In Northern Ireland it was alleged that Sinn Fein's head of security had worked as an agent for the British government under the codename 'Stakeknife'.

19.5.03

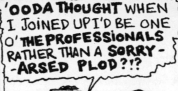

Eurobushvision

Britain's entry to the Eurovision Song Contest gained a dazzling nul points. Meanwhile Bush embarked on a global victory tour, calling at the G8 Summit in Evian, the Israel/Palestine 'Roadmap' Summit in Sharm El-Sheik, and winding up surrounded by loyal, howling troops in Doha, Qatar (Iraq itself being considered too dangerous).

2.6.2003